Brother André
A Saint for Today

NOVALIS

Lord, you note
trouble and grief ...

You have been the
helper of the orphan.

(Psalm 10:14)

"I doubt that this child will live," said the midwife, looking at Clothilde Foisy's tiny newborn son as he struggled to breathe. It was Saturday, August 9, 1845. The baby's parents decided to baptize him right away. They fetched some water and chose a name for the child. "Alfred, I baptize you in the name of the Father, and of the Son, and of the Holy Spirit," the baby's father, Isaac Bessette, said in a solemn voice as he poured water on the infant's forehead. As it turned out, this fragile baby, born in St-Grégoire d'Iberville, would live to the age of 91!

Jobs were scarce in Lower Canada, as Québec was called at that time. At the age of four, little Alfred started moving from place to place with his family in a way that would mark his youth. First, the family, now with ten children, moved to Farnham, a town that was growing quickly. There, his father, a carpenter by trade, hoped to find work. One winter's day in 1855, he and his eldest son went logging in the woods. Despite his experience felling trees, he miscalculated and a huge tree fell on him. He died that same night, February 20, and was buried two days later.

With great courage, his widow, Clothilde, became responsible for the whole family. The youngest child was barely a year old. She showed special attention to little Alfred, whose health was still delicate. Step by step, she led him into her deep faith. "You have a Father in heaven who is watching over you," she would say to him. "You can trust him. And I'll tell you a secret: you also have a very good friend up there, someone who was a carpenter, like your papa, and who was very close to Jesus. His name is Saint Joseph. Make him your friend: he will always be there to help you."

But raising her large family on her own proved to be too much for Clothilde. She died of tuberculosis only two years after her husband's death. In later years, Brother André would say of her, "I rarely prayed for my mother, but I often prayed to her."

By this time, the older children were able to find work and look after themselves. An aunt, Marie-Rosalie, who lived in Saint-Césaire, took in Alfred. This is where he prepared for his First Communion, spending two months learning the basics of the Catholic faith.

He received Holy Communion
from Father André Provençal,
who gave him a small missal
to mark this important day.

Although Alfred did not know
how to read, he would use
the missal to pray the stations
of the cross by contemplating
the illustrations.

"Foxes have holes, and
birds of the air have nests;

but the Son of Man has
nowhere to lay his head."

(Matthew 8:20)

Then Aunt Marie-Rosalie's husband, Timothée Nadeau, decided to emigrate to California, where gold had been found. So Alfred went to live with the mayor, François (Louis) Ouimet, a farmer. This generous man was the first person to notice signs of piety in Alfred that were out of the ordinary. He did not eat dessert; he wore a hair shirt made of an old chain; and he prayed. For hours! With an old crucifix that Mr. Ouimet had bought at a flea market, Alfred set up a small chapel in a corner of the barn.

Despite his poor health, Alfred tried
his hand at many trades:
shoemaker, blacksmith, tinsmith,
baker. Finally, in the summer of
1863, like thousands of French
Canadians, he went to the United
States, hoping to find work in the
textile mills of New England. But
the working conditions were
terrible, even for a healthy man:
twelve hours a day, six days a week,
in a noisy and dusty environment,
in extreme heat or cold. Four years
later, he returned to Canada. Again
he roamed from place to place,
looking for work: Sutton, Farnham,
Saint-Césaire…

Alfred was now 22 years old, and on the surface his life seemed to be a failure: poor health, no education, no career. What could he build his life on?

On his family? His brothers and sisters were spread all over, on both sides of the Canadian border.

On his wealth? He didn't even have a savings account.

On his skills? He didn't know how to read or write, and his poor health prevented him from doing jobs that were physically demanding.

For him, the choice was clear.
He would build his life on God:

the God whose presence
he had always felt,

the God towards whom he felt
so intensely drawn,

the God he wanted to serve
with all his might,

the God he enjoyed meeting
during his long hours of prayer.

Providence had placed on his path a man who would play a key role in Alfred's life: Father André Provençal, pastor of the parish of Saint-Césaire from 1850 to 1889. This enterprising man had worked to set up a convent school to educate young girls and a trade school for boys. The boys' school was run by the Congregation of Holy Cross, which had arrived in Lower Canada in 1847 and was already established in Montréal.

Father Provençal noticed how prayerful young Alfred was. The priest often saw the boy at church, completely absorbed in prayer. "It's clear that God is calling this young man to religious life," he thought. He spoke to Alfred about this vocation, explaining that members of religious orders are not all teachers: many practise a trade or serve others.

Alfred felt that this was what he had always wanted to do. On November 22, 1870, carrying a letter of recommendation from his pastor, he went to Notre-Dame College in Montréal. In Father Provençal's letter, the master of novices read, "I am sending you a saint."

It is no longer I who
live, but it is Christ
who lives in me.

And the life I now
live in the flesh

I live by faith in
the Son of God,

who loved me and gave
himself for me.

(Galatians 2:20)

So he entered the Holy Cross community. For him, everything had changed and nothing had changed. Everything had changed because he was part of a new family, the Congregation of Holy Cross. He was also in a new environment where everything, from the accommodations to the daily schedule and activities, centred on the spiritual life.

On the other hand, nothing had changed: he kept deepening his relationship with God and with his good friend Saint Joseph. Alfred went on doing small chores as caretaker, porter, infirmary attendant. Because of his weak stomach, he ate very little, which limited his physical strength – so much so that, at the end of the novitiate, the community considered having him leave.

In the end, the new master of novices, Father Amédée Guy, decided to keep him, saying, "If this young man ever becomes unable to work, at least he'll be very good at praying!" On February 2, 1874, at the age of 28, Alfred Bessette made his perpetual vows and took a new name. He chose the name "Brother André" in honour of his former pastor, Father Provençal.

Sickly, shy and without any education, Brother André should have lived a life of total obscurity. His existence should have filled a mere two or three lines of the Congregation's history.

How did he become for thousands of people "Good Brother André," a man whom English newspapers called "The miracle man of Montréal" even while he was still alive?

Brother André never sought
glory or fame. He strongly
objected to any miracles being
attributed to him. For him, all
these marvels were the work
of God and God's servant
Saint Joseph. "I am only
Saint Joseph's little dog,"
he liked to say.

Yet this little man who
may have seemed laughable
on the human level was
a spiritual giant.

God is like lightning, always
taking the path of least resistance.
And in the soul of Brother André,
there was no trace of pride,
no selfishness. He was totally
seduced by the beauty of God,
which the cross of Jesus Christ
enabled him to discover.

By spending so many hours contemplating Christ in prayer, Brother André in some ways became the one he contemplated. Like Christ, he was filled with a deep compassion for those who suffered in any way.

And so God made of him a special instrument through which God could reveal his active presence in the lives of those who were suffering.

"Come to me, all you that are weary and are carrying heavy burdens,

and I will give you rest."

(Matthew 11:28)

D riven by this deep compassion, and in spite of his very busy schedule, Brother André managed to find time to visit the sick. He would listen to them, talk to them, even make them laugh. Above all, he would invite them to trust in and pray to Saint Joseph. As a token of this trust, he would give them a medal of Saint Joseph or a small bottle of the oil that

burned before the statue of
Saint Joseph in the chapel,
and would recommend that
they rub some of the oil
on their skin.

After his visits, people would
feel better; some were even
fully healed. As the news spread,
people started coming to the
college and asking for him.

Individuals became small groups, and small groups became crowds. Some parents of the students at the college became concerned. What if their children became infected by all those sick people? The Superior of the college had no choice: he ordered Brother André to see his "patients" outside the school walls. But what was he to do in the winter?

A new tramway line that had just been completed went right past the college. It was decided that Brother André would meet those who came to him in a little tramway station the community had built. He used this space for ten years, until a small room and office were set up for him near the first chapel.

Brother André didn't keep a record of the cures he performed. For one thing, he could hardly read or write. But most importantly, he avoided anything that hinted of a personality cult.

On the other hand, it can't be denied that he did give their health back to thousands of people who were suffering from various ailments: rheumatism, arthritis, cancer, heart disease, asthma, and injuries from serious accidents.

In 1922, Colonel G. George Ham, a Protestant, wrote, "One can say that, during the last decade, at least 30,000 people expressed their gratitude to Brother André for the help they received from him, either through physical or spiritual cure."

Most of the miracle accounts have come to us through direct witnesses. Here are four of their testimonials.

First
testimonial

I am a doctor. Among my patients were the students of Notre-Dame College. My first contacts with Brother André were difficult, to say the least.

It all started the day I sent a young student with a very high fever to the infirmary. To my surprise, I saw him soon after playing with his friends. "You must go to bed," I ordered him. "You're sick." "I'm not sick anymore," he replied. "Brother André healed me!" I checked, and in fact the fever had vanished. "Just a coincidence," I thought. "But this uneducated Brother should mind his own business and stop pretending to be a doctor!"

From that time on, I was his declared enemy. I would criticize him openly and scorn him by calling him "the greasy brother" in front of everyone. To my mind, he was not only incompetent, but a dangerous charlatan claiming to heal people with medals and oil.

*All that changed when my wife began
to hemorrhage severely and neither
I nor my colleagues could stop the
bleeding. I could see my beloved wife
getting weaker every day. She was
confined to her bed.*

One morning, she said to me,
"My dear, only one person can
heal me: Brother André." You can
imagine my reaction: "Never!
I will never humble myself before that
charlatan!" But I loved my wife
more than anything. So I swallowed
my pride and called Brother André.
He agreed to come and see her.

On the way to my home, he told me,
"Your wife will not die." The moment
she saw him, the bleeding stopped.
She was healed ... and so was I,
from my pride and my lack of faith.

Joseph-Albin Charette, *M.D.*

Second testimonial

*I*n 1910, I was working for the
Canadian Pacific Railway.
One day, some other employees and
I were moving huge blocks of marble.

*Suddenly, three or four blocks fell
on me, crushing my feet and lower
legs. The bones were broken and
the muscles torn. After six months
in hospital, I could hardly walk,
even with crutches: my legs could
no longer support me.*

With great difficulty, I climbed up
to the small chapel of Mount Royal.
Brother André listened to my story.
Then, after praying, he rubbed my
legs with the oil of Saint Joseph and
said to me, "Throw away your
crutches: you are healed."

*Since then, I have been able to walk,
and don't even need a cane!*

Martin Hannon, *labourer*

Third testimonial

I witnessed at least two miracles.

First, Brother André healed me from pneumonia after nothing else worked. In his room he was also tending a man whose leg had become gangrenous. It smelled awful and a yellowish pus oozed out of it.

A few days later, I came back to the Oratory with a friend to make a thanksgiving offering. My friend didn't believe in Brother André. In fact, he didn't believe in anything. I brought him to see the man with the gangrenous leg. "If this man is healed," my friend said, "I'll be forced to believe!"

Not long afterwards, we went to the Oratory again. That same man greeted us, standing on his two legs, fully cured. My friend was speechless. He went to pray in the chapel. "We brought a sinner back to faith," I told Brother André. And he answered, "You, and me, and Saint Joseph."

Leon, *labourer*

Fourth testimonial

*M*ore and more people were coming to the chapel that was completed in 1910. Brother André asked his Superior, Father Dion, if a priest could be made available to them. Father Dion asked me if I would take on this role.

At that time, I was 33 years old and had had to stop teaching because of problems with my eyesight. I couldn't even read my breviary anymore.
So I went to Brother André and told him, "The priest they are sending you is practically blind. But I can still hear confessions and celebrate Mass."

A few weeks later, I had to tell him, "Brother André, it's getting worse. Now I can barely read the large print in the missal. I don't know how much longer I'll be able to celebrate Mass." He simply answered, "Father Clément, Saint Joseph needs you. Tomorrow morning, pray your breviary, then come to celebrate Mass."

*The next morning, to my great
surprise, I could easily read
the small print in my breviary.
That summer of 1910, we welcomed
200,000 pilgrims!*

Fr. Adolphe Clément, *c.s.c.*

"The crowds
followed Jesus; and
he welcomed them,

and spoke to them about
the kingdom of God,

and healed those who
needed healing."

(Luke 9:11)

Jesus performed many miracles during his life, as did many of the saints. One definition of "miracle" could be *an amazing and free sign of God's love for someone who believes in him.*

A miracle must be astonishing and must not be able to be explained by science. A miracle is free: God performs it when he wants and for whom he wants.

And a miracle is possible only when there is faith. "The good Lord is good," Brother André used to say. "These healings do good to the one healed and to those who hear about it. This helps them grow in faith."

The two aspects of a miracle are therefore God's compassion for human suffering and faith in God's presence in our lives. Brother André prayed the stations of the cross every day because he saw in Jesus the God who shared in our suffering and who meets us in our suffering today.

Joseph Pichette, a friend and confidant of Brother André's, wrote, "I never brought a sick person to Brother André without that person returning home enriched. Some were healed, and others died some time later, but Brother André had brought them peace of mind."

We ponder your
steadfast love,
O God,

in the midst
of your temple.

Let Mount Zion
be glad.

(Psalm 48:9, 11)

From the time he arrived in Montréal, Brother André loved going up the mountain in front of the college to pray. He found the silence, the tranquillity, and the beautiful scenery conducive to prayer.

In 1896, the Congregation bought the land so that no noisy or inappropriate business could be built there. But Brother André had another project in mind. He dreamed of building a chapel on the mountain so that people could come and pray in that wonderful setting. Thanks to support from friends and volunteers, his dream became a reality. In 1910, the construction of the first chapel was completed.

But as the crowds grew larger
and larger, plans were made
for a basilica. The crypt
was finished in 1917.

The stock market crash
of 1929 meant that further
work on the basilica itself had
to be postponed. Still, it was
ready in time to welcome
the body of Brother André,
who died on January 6, 1937.

A million people came
to pay their last respects.

Today, over two million people
come each year to pray at the
Oratory of Saint Joseph –
not only because the building
and surroundings are beautiful,
but because visitors feel a
Presence there: the Presence
of a merciful God.

Brother André was both a witness
and a servant to that Presence.

Bibliography

Burton, Katherine. *Brother André of Mount Royal*. Notre Dame, Indiana: Ave Maria Press, 1952.

Dubuc, Jean-Guy. *Brother André*. Montréal: Fides, 1999.

Grenon, Hector. *Le frère André raconté par Hector Grenon*. Montréal: Stanké, 1981.

Lachance, Micheline. *Le frère André*. Montréal: Les Éditions de l'Homme, 1979.

Nadeau, Denise. *Le frère André*. Montréal: Lidec, 1993.